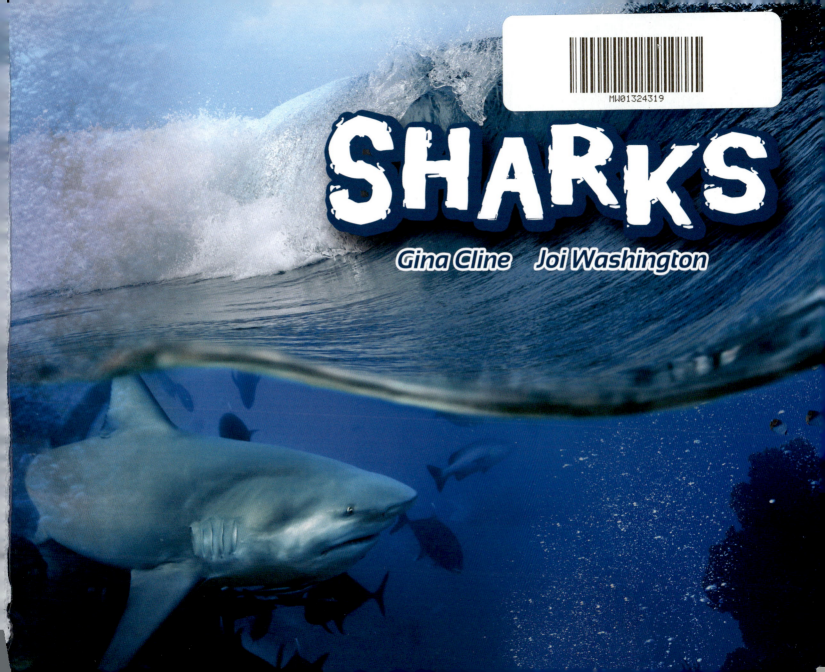

SHARKS

Gina Cline Joi Washington

Reef Shark

This is a shark.

Nurse Shark

This is a shark, too.

All of these are sharks.

Some sharks are big.
This shark is as big as a boat.

This is an egg.

Dogfish Shark Eggs

Some sharks have eggs.

Dogfish Shark Egg

There are baby sharks in the eggs.

Lemon Shark

Some sharks don't have eggs. They have babies.

Some sharks will eat the babies.

Reef Sharks

Some sharks live with lots of sharks.

Sand Tiger Shark

Some sharks don't.

Some sharks live with fish.

The fish eat what the shark eats.

CAMOUFLAGE

Sharks look like where they live.

Some sharks look like the water.

Zebra Shark

Some sharks look like the rocks.

Nurse Shark

Some sharks look like sand.

FOOD

Reef Sharks

Sharks have to eat.

Hammerhead Shark

All sharks eat fish.

Many sharks eat crabs.

Many sharks will eat squid.

Some sharks eat seals.

Some sharks will eat turtles.

Some sharks eat birds.

Bull Shark

Great White Shark

Tiger Shark

Not many sharks eat people. These can.

Sharks Live Here

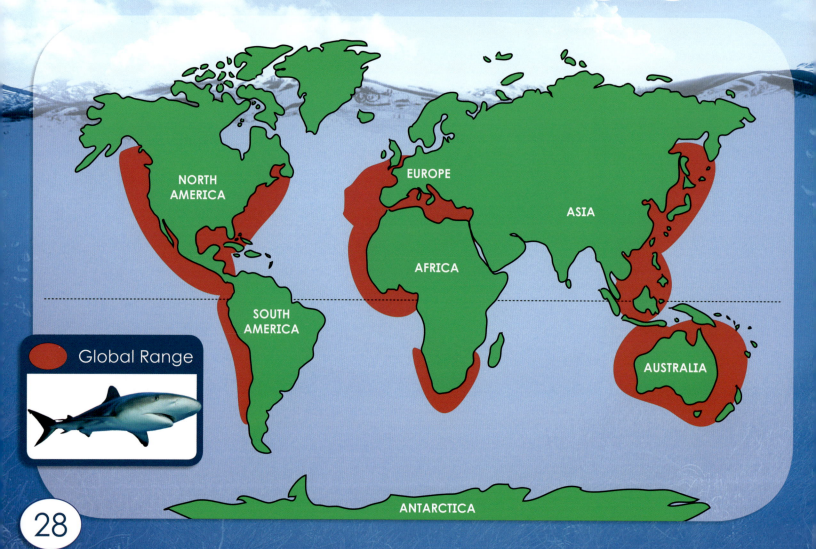

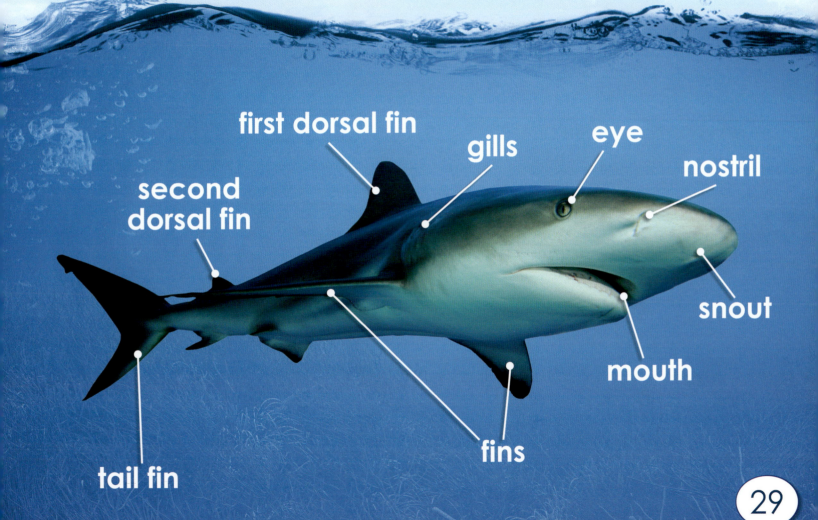

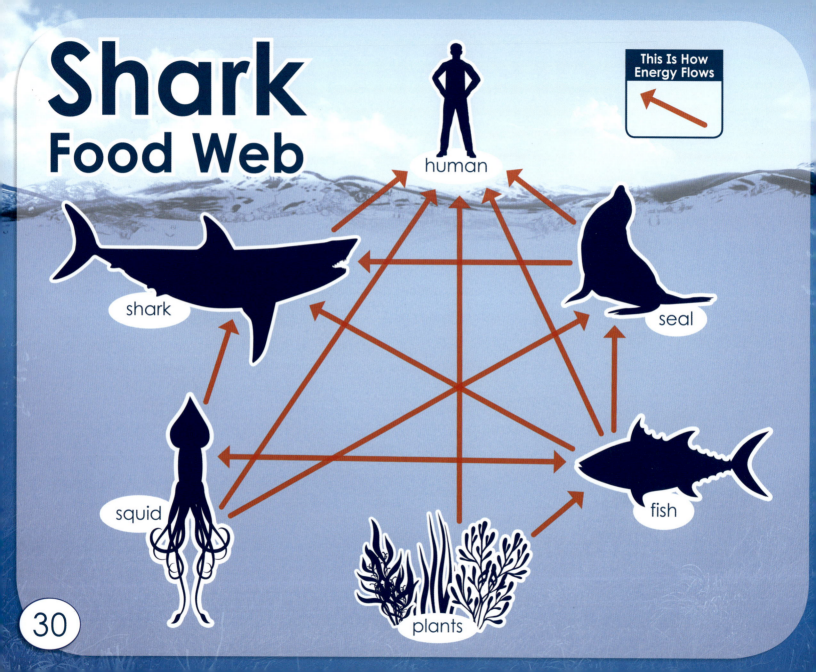

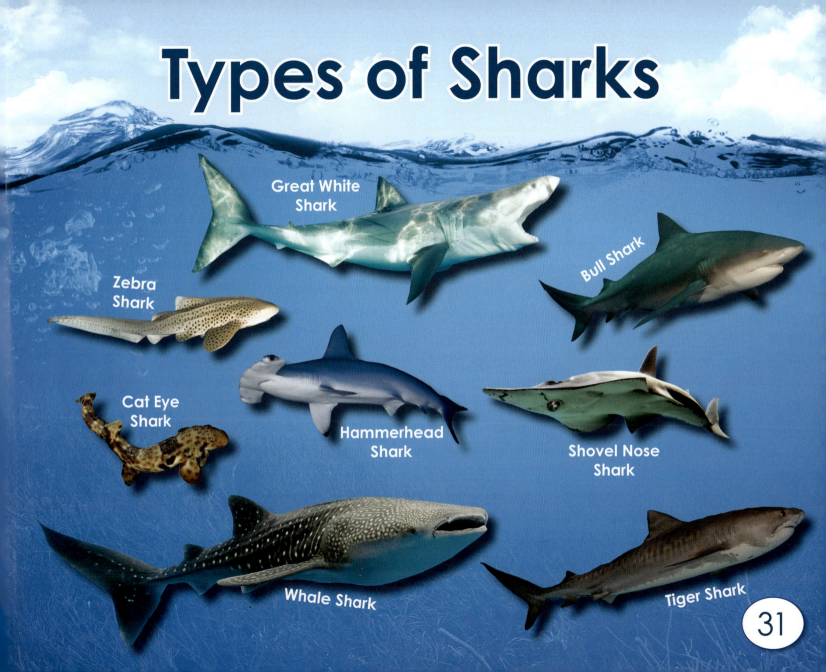

Power Words
How many can you read?

a	baby	have	live	of	they	what
all	big	in	look	some	this	where
an	can	is	lots	the	to	will
are	don't	like	many	there	too	with
as	eat	little	not	these		